Letters of a Father to His Son Jeremiah—

A Spiritual Journey to Meaning, Purpose, and Identity

The
Freeman
Institute
FOR INTEGRATIVE RESEARCH

Eric J. Freeman, PhD

The Freeman Institute

FOR INTEGRATIVE RESEARCH

Copyright © 2025 by Eric J. Freeman
All rights reserved.

Published by
The Freeman Institute for Integrative Research
201 Columbia Mall Blvd.
Columbia, SC 29223

ISBN 979-8-9929512-3-3

First Edition

The Freeman Institute for Integrative Research

This book is a product of *The Freeman Institute for Integrative Research* —an interdisciplinary initiative committed to bridging rigorous theological study with real-world application. The Institute exists to make doctrine accessible, elevate historically marginalized voices, and provide believers with spiritually formative resources that speak to the challenges of contemporary life.

Letters of a Father to His Son Jeremiah—A Spiritual Journey to Meaning, Purpose, and Identity reflects the Institute's mission to offer theologically grounded, emotionally honest tools that nurture both spiritual growth and prophetic engagement.

To learn more or access additional resources, visit:

EricJFreeman.com

To the one I could not reach,
and to the many still listening—
may these words find you when you are ready, and
remind you that you were always known.

"You have seen well, for I am watching over My word to perform it."
—Jeremiah 1:12

Table of Contents

BEFORE YOU READ THE FIRST LETTER

Introduction

These are not letters of certainty.

They are letters of *return*—to the quiet places where fear and faith wrestle, where calling feels like ache, and where love waits longer than most people think it should.

I wrote them first in silence.

They were never intended for publication.

They were meant for one person—someone I love deeply, someone I cannot currently reach. But in the years of praying, waiting, and writing, I realized: these words were never just for one heart. They belong to many.

So if you've found this book, there's probably a reason.

You may be carrying a call you never asked for.

You may be searching for your name beneath the labels you've picked up or been given.

You may be tired of speaking when no one seems to

hear.

Or maybe you're just beginning to sense that something sacred is stirring inside you—and you're wondering whether you're worthy of it.

These letters are for you.

They come from the voice of a spiritual father— sometimes poetic, sometimes prophetic, always honest. They are rooted in the call of the prophet Jeremiah, but written to any soul who's ever asked: *Am I really called? Can I carry this? What if I'm not enough?*

The narrative is epistolary.

Each chapter is a letter.

They were written over time, never mailed, and eventually discovered—like seeds folded into the corner of an old coat, still waiting to bloom.

You don't need to read them all at once.

Let them meet you where you are. One letter a day. One letter a week. One letter in the moment when you feel like giving up. They are not linear—they are circular. They come back around when you need them most.

And though they are addressed to "Jeremiah," that name carries meaning, not limitation.

Jeremiah stands for the called. The reluctant. The courageous. The ones who cry and speak anyway. The ones who walk quietly with the fire of God shut up in their bones.

So take your time.

Read slowly.

Return as needed.

My only hope is that these words will remind you:

You are not alone.

You are not forgotten.

You were known before you were formed.

And the call on your life is not performance—it is presence.

If you've been looking for a sign to keep going, this just may be it.

LETTER 0: IF THESE WORDS EVER FIND YOU

A Preface to the Letters

My Beloved Jeremiah,

I don't know if these words will ever reach you. I've imagined, more times than I care to admit, what it would be like if they did—if your eyes one day found these pages, if your heart opened even a little to hear what I've carried all this time. But imagination is not certainty. And love, when it is real, must learn to live with silence.

So I make no assumptions.

This letter does not ask for a reply. It is not bait or burden. It is simply what remains when a voice still believes in what it once began to say.

Sometimes love must speak—not to be heard, but to be *honest*.

I've written these letters not because I have answers, but because I have *hope*.

Not because I expect you to follow my steps, but

because I believe there is something sacred in remembering the steps that led me here.

I didn't write to convince you.

I didn't write to rescue you.

I wrote because love must leave light on the path—just in case someone ever decides to come home.

There are things a parent carries long after the conversation ends. And some truths, too deep for arguments and too fragile for speeches, must be written down quietly and laid aside, like folded garments, waiting for their season.

This is that kind of writing.

What follows are letters—some tender, some hard-won—written in the voice of a father to a child named for the prophet Jeremiah.

They are not sermons. Not instructions. Not polished arguments. They are fragments of a fire I could not put out. Words that rose in me over time. Prayers, really, more than positions.

Each one circles a single question: *What does it mean to be called, and not run?*

You will see scripture in these pages, especially the first chapter of Jeremiah. You will hear echoes of my own wrestlings with fear, identity, purpose, and the long silence that sometimes follows faith.

But you'll also hear this: I never stopped believing you were meant for more.

I don't know when these words will find you—if in youth or age, in confusion or clarity. But I have prayed that they meet you at the right moment, in the right way, even if my voice is long gone from your memory.

Sometimes truth waits in silence until we are ready to hear it.

Sometimes love travels quietly through time, wrapped in paper, buried in pages, until the soil is soft enough for planting.

If nothing else, may you know this: there was never a day I didn't hope for your wholeness. Never a day I didn't believe there was something holy in you— something worth waiting for, something worth writing for.

And so I place these letters here—without demand,
without fanfare.

Like seeds scattered in hope.

If they take root, if they grow, if they give light or
comfort or strength—then let it be the Lord's doing,
and let it be marvelous in your eyes.

And if not . . . still, I am at peace.

Because love has spoken. And that is enough.

May your eyes be clear and your spirit steady.

May courage find you gently and rise in you fiercely.

And may you never forget:

You were known before you were named,
and loved long before you ever knew it.

—*Abba*

PART 1

KNOWN BEFORE NAMED

The Foundation of Identity and Calling

LETTER 1: BEFORE YOU WERE YOU

A Father's Letters to His Child, Named for the Prophet

My Beloved Jeremiah,

Before you were you, *you were Mine.*

Not in the sense of ownership, but of origin. Before your voice found its sound, before your body took its shape, before your name was spoken on anyone's lips—you were already known. Not vaguely. Not conceptually. But intimately. Personally. Eternally.

There is something older than your questions. Older than your fear. Older even than your first breath. And that something is love.

The kind that does not wait for you to become something worthy, but names you *beloved* from the beginning. The kind that does not rely on performance, perfection, or even presence to remain true.

You were seen before you were visible.

Chosen before you were ready.

Held before you were ever held.

But somewhere along the way, we forget.

The world teaches us to see ourselves in fragments—in achievements, in mistakes, in comparisons, in shadows. We begin to believe that we are the sum of what we've survived or the echo of what others have said. We let fear rewrite the narrative. We let shame interrupt the melody.

And soon, what we *feel* becomes louder than what God *declared*.

I've seen it happen in others. I've felt it in myself. The quiet unraveling of identity when the world hands you names that do not fit: *Too much. Not enough. Too late. Not ready.* And we wear them like coats, even when they don't keep us warm.

But none of those names are older than the One who called you *Mine*.

Long before you knew your name, *God knew your nature*.

Before you could form a question, He had already formed a calling. Before you could reach for meaning, He had already spoken purpose over your

2

life. You were not an accident. You were not a gamble. You were not a late thought in the mind of God. You were *appointed*.

And what God appoints, He does not abandon. The pain hasn't undone it. The silence hasn't canceled it. Even the choices you regret have not disqualified you. The calling on your life is not built on your consistency—it is built on *God's constancy*. You didn't earn it, so you can't erase it.

You were chosen in a voice that spoke before time, and no other voice gets the final word.

When you live from that truth—not just visit it, but *abide* in it—everything begins to shift.

You stop striving to earn what was already yours.

You stop shrinking to fit into rooms you were born to reshape.

You stop measuring your value by the reactions of others and start living as one already *received*.

Confidence becomes quieter, but deeper. You no longer need the applause to confirm your assignment. You walk differently—not with arrogance, but with authority. You move through fear, not because it vanishes, but because it no longer gets to decide who you are.

You've been named already. Claimed already. Sent already.

And when you truly believe that, the pressure lifts. Not the responsibility—but the pressure. Because now you understand: your task is not to prove your worth, but to walk in it.

So go back—not to relive the past, but to *remember your beginning.*

Not the beginning marked by time, but the one marked by eternity.

The one where God saw you and said, *Yes.*

The one where nothing had to be earned, and everything was already enough.

That beginning is not behind you. It's *within* you. And every time you return to it, you are not retreating—you are being *restored.*

So walk forward, child.

Walk with your head lifted—not because you are

certain, but because you are known.

Walk, not as one trying to become someone, but as one already *sent*.

You were not a mistake.

You were a word spoken in love.

And that Word still lives in you.

With all my heart,

—*Abba*

LETTER 2: THE FACES THAT SCARE US

A Father's Letters to His Child, Named for the Prophet

My Beloved Jeremiah,

There is a quiet power in a human face.

You can sense it in a raised brow, a furrowed forehead, a glance that lingers too long—or not long enough. We were made for connection, so we learn early to read expressions like scripture. We search eyes for approval, tone for acceptance. And when we don't find it, something in us folds.

You know what I mean.

You've felt the shift in a room when your voice enters. You've watched a face tighten when you speak the truth. You've tasted the silence that follows a stand you didn't want to take, but had to. It doesn't take yelling to intimidate someone. Sometimes, all it takes is *a look*.

And if we are not careful, those looks become commands.

We shrink. We edit. We adjust. We begin to make our decisions in response to reactions—living our lives not from within, but from the outside in.

That's why the Lord said it so plainly: *"Do not be afraid of their faces."*

He didn't say, *Don't be afraid of armies.* Or *Don't be afraid of arguments.*

He said *faces*—because God knows where fear lives. Fear doesn't always shout from mountaintops. Sometimes it stares back at you from across a table, across a sanctuary, across a memory. It speaks without speaking. And it can paralyze the strongest voice if left unchecked.

Why did God need to say it?

Because He knew you would be sent to speak things that wouldn't sit well. He knew your courage would be tested not just by opposition, but by expression. And He knew how easy it would be to start preaching to approval instead of truth.

Do not be afraid of their faces.

It sounds simple. But it's not. It's holy instruction—
for prophets, for preachers, for anyone called to
speak light into rooms that have grown accustomed
to the dark.

There's a slow erosion that happens when we start
living for approval.

It doesn't begin with compromise. It begins with
hesitation.

We hesitate before we speak. We hesitate before we
stand. We start editing our convictions to avoid
discomfort. Not because we don't believe the truth,
but because we're not sure the room can handle it—
and we're not sure we can handle the room.

So we adjust. Soften. Shrink.

And somewhere along the way, we trade the voice
God gave us for a version shaped by expectation. A
version calibrated to avoid rejection, to win
applause, to keep peace at the cost of integrity.

But approval is a moving target. You hit it one day,
only to find it's shifted the next.

You cannot anchor your identity in a crowd's reaction and expect to stand when the storm comes. That's why courage doesn't begin with volume—it begins with vision.

Not *how* you see, but *whose* gaze you live under. The face you seek must not be theirs. It must be His.

Only the eyes of God will love you enough to correct you, stay with you, send you, and still call you *Mine*.

Can you imagine the freedom of living for *One*?

Not for applause.

Not for nods.

Not even for understanding.

But for the One whose face has never flinched when looking at you. The One whose gaze does not waver with your weakness or shift with the trends. The One whose eyes saw you before anyone else did— and still said, *Go*.

What would happen if *that* was the face you sought?

You would no longer need permission to speak what is true. You would stop performing, stop hiding, stop asking people to tell you who you are. You would lift your eyes above the room, above the reaction, above the fear—and see the face of the One who called you.

And in that gaze, you would find what no crowd can give:

Security. Clarity. Courage.

Because when you live for the audience of One, you are never outnumbered.

So let me say it again, as the Lord once said to you:

Do not be afraid of their faces.

Do not let a glance undo your calling. Do not let silence steal your authority. Do not let rejection make you forget the One who already received you.

Lift your eyes.

Above the stare. Above the smirk. Above the silence.

Lift your eyes until you see the face that has never turned from you.

And when you see it—when you feel the warmth of
that gaze upon your life—let that be your anchor.

Let it be your courage.

Walk forward in truth, even when the room shifts.

Speak when you are sent, even if no one seems
ready.

Love fiercely, even when the faces do not reflect it
back.

You are not sent to please them.

You are sent to be faithful to *Him*.

And His face is always toward you.

With unshaken love,

—*Abba*

LETTER 3: WHAT'S IN A NAME

A Father's Letters to His Child, Named for the Prophet

My Beloved Jeremiah,

I did not give you a name to fill a blank space.

I gave you a name because I believed in what it could call forth.

Because I knew that one day you would wonder who you are—and that your name might whisper the answer back to you when nothing else could.

Names carry more than syllables. They carry *intention*. A name is a kind of prophecy. It doesn't just tell others what to call you—it reminds you who you were becoming, even before you could articulate the question.

I named you not for popularity, but for purpose. Not for fashion, but for fire.

I named you for the one who wept and spoke anyway. The one who stood alone and still told the truth. The one who knew what it meant to carry the weight of a word bigger than himself.

There is power in being named.

Not just in sound, but in meaning. In memory. In mystery.

When God names someone in scripture, it is never casual. Names are covenant. They signal identity, but they also reveal destiny. Abram becomes Abraham. Jacob becomes Israel. Simon becomes Peter. And every shift in name points to a deeper truth: *You are not who you were—but who God is calling you to become.*

And sometimes, calling is hidden in plain sight— tucked inside the name we've grown used to, waiting to be rediscovered when the time is right.

The world will try to rename you.

It will label you by your failure, your silence, your struggle. It will call you weak when you weep, difficult when you dissent, lost when you walk away from what is false. But those are not your names. And they do not belong to you.

You were named before the world had a chance to redefine you.

You were called before they could categorize you.

When the ground beneath you feels unsteady, remembering your name can be a lifeline.

Not the name others gave you when they were angry.

Not the name you gave yourself when you were afraid.

But the name spoken over you when God said, *"Before I formed you, I knew you."*

In seasons of rejection, your name reminds you that you were received before you were refused.

In moments of confusion, it brings you back to who you are beneath the questions.

And when fear rises—when the silence lingers and the faces grow cold—your name becomes a thread tying you to the One who has not changed His mind about you.

You were not named by accident.

You were named with authority.

And your name still knows the way home.

Somewhere along the way, we all pick up names that were never ours to carry.

Too broken.

Too sensitive.

Too late.

Too much.

We wear them like second skin. Not because we believe them at first, but because they're repeated often enough—spoken by others, reinforced by silence, echoed in our own thoughts.

Eventually, we forget where the lie ends and we begin.

But child, listen to me: those are not your names. You are not your wounds. You are not your worst day. You are not the name whispered in anger, or the label attached to your survival.

You are the one God knew.

The one God formed.

The one God named—not for what the world
would say about you, but for what He saw in you
from the beginning.

If you've forgotten who you are, this is your
invitation to *remember*.

If you've been called everything but beloved, this is
your permission to reclaim the truth.

Your name is still intact.

It's been waiting.

Your name is not just something to remember.

It is something to *walk in*.

It is not only a reflection of who you were—it is
a *signal* of who you're becoming. A quiet
commissioning. A sacred tether. A word spoken in
heaven that still has work to do on earth.

So walk in it.

Even when you don't feel worthy.

Even when the world gets loud and the way gets
long.

Even when no one else remembers what you were
called.

Because your name does not belong to the
moment—it belongs to the mission.
And the One who gave it has not taken it back.
Walk forward with your head lifted.
Not because you're perfect, but because you
were *named*.
And names like yours don't disappear. They *echo*.
With all the grace I've been given,
—*Abba*

LETTER 4: THE FIRE AND THE FRUSTRATION

A Father's Letters to His Child, Named for the Prophet

My Beloved Jeremiah,

There is a kind of fire that doesn't warm you—
it *won't let you rest.*

It flickers beneath your ribs and settles deep in your
bones. You didn't ask for it. You didn't light it
yourself. But there it is—burning, calling, pressing.
Not with rage, but with weight. Not with heat
alone, but with purpose. And it changes everything.

It interrupts your comfort.

It rewrites your plans.

It refuses to stay silent.

And sometimes, it doesn't feel like a blessing.

It feels like *burden.*

The world often romanticizes calling—as if it's a
dream you choose. But anyone who's truly been
called knows better. It's not always noble. It's not
always clear. It's not always welcome. And there will

be days when you wonder if it would have been easier not to feel anything at all.

That's why the prophet said, *"If I try to hold it in, it becomes like fire shut up in my bones, and I am weary with holding it in—indeed, I cannot."*

He wasn't boasting. He was *breaking*.

This was not the fire of inspiration. It was the ache of obedience. The cost of carrying a word you cannot unhear. The exhaustion of being faithful in a world that rewards performance but punishes truth. You will want to quit sometimes—not because you don't love God, but because the fire won't let you rest. You will feel weary from the waiting, the speaking, the repeating of what no one seems ready to receive. And yet, you will keep going. Not because it feels good, but because the fire leaves you no other honest choice.

Obedience isn't always a door that opens to peace. Sometimes it's the fire you learn to *live with*.

What no one tells you about calling is that it will break your heart.

Not because something is wrong with you, but because something is right with your vision. The more clearly you see what *should be*, the more deeply you'll feel what *is not*. And that gap—that holy tension—will grieve you.

Frustration is not failure. It is evidence that your heart has started to beat in rhythm with God's. When you are called, you do not get to look away. You don't get to stand safely at a distance. You feel what God feels. You mourn what He mourns. You love people who don't love you back. You speak to a world that seems to plug its ears. And still—you stay.

That's what makes your frustration sacred. Not because it is pleasant, but because it is *participation* in God's compassion.

The ache is not your enemy. It's a sign you're still tender, still listening, still *in it*.

Do not mistake your frustration for failure.

The presence of fire does not mean you're doing something wrong—it often means you're finally getting close to something holy. Frustration doesn't mean you've lost the way. Sometimes it means you've stepped more fully into it.

God never promised the fire would be comfortable. But He did promise it would be *purifying*.

You are not being consumed. You are being refined. The fire is not there to punish you—it is there to sustain you when applause fades, when answers don't come, when you wonder if your voice still matters. It is not a punishment. It is a *provision*.

So let the fire shape you. Let it burn away what was never meant to stay. Let it leave behind only what is durable enough to carry the weight of truth.

This is how prophets are formed—not in comfort, but in consecration.

So carry the fire.

Not with shame. Not with fear. But with reverence. Let it teach you how to endure. Let it shape your voice, your heart, your posture. Let it remind you— on the days you feel empty or unseen—that you are *still burning*, and therefore *still alive* to the work of God within you.

You don't need to extinguish the fire to be at peace.

You need to trust that the One who lit it is the One who sustains it.

You are not alone in this.

Many have walked with the ache. Many still do. But this fire—this holy weight—is part of your consecration. It's not proof of your weakness. It's evidence of your calling.

So when the weariness comes, don't run.

Let the fire speak for you. Let it keep you. Let it form you.

Because when everything else fades, it will still be there—

shut up in your bones, whispering, *You were made for this.*

With enduring strength,

—*Abba*

PART 2

WRESTLING WITH THE CALL

Fear, Resistance, and the Slow Growth of Obedience

LETTER 5: WHEN PURPOSE HURTS

A Father's Letters from the Wilderness of Calling

My Beloved Jeremiah,

No one tells you that purpose can break your heart. Not because you've done something wrong—but because you finally started doing something *right*.

There's a kind of pain that doesn't come from failure or rebellion, but from obedience. A quiet ache that rises when you say yes to God and find yourself more alone than before, more exposed than expected, more burdened than blessed.

This isn't the suffering of consequence. It's the suffering of calling.

It's what happens when you carry something sacred in a world that prefers safety. When you speak truth into silence and feel the silence grow deeper. When you love with open hands and still watch people walk away.

And it hurts—not because you weren't ready, but because *you were*.

We don't expect purpose to feel like this.

We expect clarity. Confirmation. A sense of momentum. We expect that saying yes to God will open doors, settle questions, and surround us with support.

But sometimes, it does the opposite.

Sometimes, purpose isolates you.

It confuses people who once stood close to you.

It exposes insecurities you didn't know you carried.

It introduces you to resistance from places you thought would cheer.

And so you begin to ask: *Did I misunderstand the call? Did I move too soon? Did I make this up?*

No, child. You didn't misunderstand it.

You *embodied* it.

And that's why it hurts.

This is the pain of the prophet—not the one who is lost, but the one who sees too clearly. Not the one who missed the path, but the one who walks it with eyes open.

It doesn't mean you've strayed.

It means you've stepped into something real.

If it hurts, let it hurt.

You don't have to pretend it doesn't. You don't have to spiritualize your sorrow or explain away your ache. You're allowed to feel what you feel. You're allowed to cry even while you're called. You're allowed to be faithful *and* wounded at the same time.

This pain is not weakness. It's evidence that your heart is still open—still tender to the movement of God, still alive to the suffering of others, still sensitive to what's broken.

Prophets aren't numb. They're *exposed*.

And grief is not a betrayal of your calling. It's part of it.

So don't run from the sorrow. Sit with it if you must. Weep with it. Pray through it. Let it shape your prayers, your pace, your posture. And when you've gathered enough strength to rise again, do so—not because the pain has vanished, but because the *call is still true*.

Even Jesus wept.

He who walked in perfect obedience—He who *was* the Word—still groaned under the weight of it. He wept at a tomb. He wept over a city. He sweat blood in the garden. He cried out on the cross.

Not because He lacked faith.

But because faith does not silence sorrow.

It *sanctifies* it.

If the Son of God could suffer and still be pleasing to the Father, then so can you.

There is no shame in your groaning. There is no guilt in your tears. There is no failure in your lament. These are not signs that you've missed the call—they are signs that you are walking in the same path He walked.

And that means you are *not alone in it*.

The One who called you is not watching from a distance. He is *with you in the grief*, familiar with suffering, acquainted with the weight of purpose. And He is not asking you to fake peace. He is offering you His presence.

So let the pain speak—not to shame you, but to shape you.

Let it deepen your compassion. Let it clarify your voice. Let it remind you that prophets don't just proclaim God's heart—they *share in it*.

And His heart is not numb.

It still breaks.

It still bleeds.

It still bears the burden of love.

You are not disqualified by this ache.

You are not less anointed because you limp.

You are not less chosen because you grieve.

You are human—and holy.

Wounded—and still walking.

Hurting—and still held.

So walk on, beloved.

Not because it doesn't hurt, but because you are *still sent*.

And the One who sent you knows exactly what it costs.

With gentleness and fire,

—*Abba*

LETTER 6: REACHING BEYOND
POPULARITY

A Father's Letters from the Wilderness of Calling

My Beloved Jeremiah,

No one starts out wanting to be popular.

You begin with a burden, a truth you cannot shake.

You speak because something holy has been planted

in you. And at first, the cost doesn't matter. But

somewhere along the way, you begin to notice the

room. You watch how people respond. You feel

which words open doors and which ones close them.

And then it happens—not as rebellion, but as

instinct.

You start editing—not the truth itself, but its edges.

You soften the sharper parts. You skip the lines that

make people uncomfortable. Not because you've

stopped believing, but because you'd rather be heard

than dismissed. You'd rather be welcomed than

avoided.

And slowly, almost imperceptibly, the message
begins to shift.
Not because you stopped loving God.
But because you started needing the people more
than you thought.
The danger isn't that you'll stop speaking.
It's that you'll start speaking only what's safe.
It happens subtly. You begin trimming the truth to
fit the room. You leave out what you were sent to
say—not because you don't believe it, but because
you're afraid of what it might cost.
And eventually, your voice loses its weight.
Not because it's gone quiet, but because it has
stopped reaching.
It no longer stretches people. It no longer
stretches *you*.
It conforms. It protects. It adapts until it becomes
acceptable—then expected—then ignored.
And a voice that was once *anointed* becomes
merely *approved*.
That is not what you were made for.

You were not called to echo what makes others comfortable. You were called to carry what makes them *awake*.

It's natural to want to be understood.

To want your intentions seen clearly, your heart interpreted charitably, your voice received with kindness.

But if you are not careful, the desire to be understood will evolve into the need to be liked.

And once that happens, purpose begins to bend.

You start asking the wrong questions:

Will they be offended? Will they still follow me? Will they think less of me if I say this, do this, live this way?

And before long, your decisions aren't shaped by calling—they're shaped by comfort and consensus.

That's how people-pleasing works.

It doesn't ask you to abandon the truth. It simply asks you to water it down—*just enough* to keep things smooth. Just enough to stay visible, palatable, unbothered.

But the gospel was never meant to go down easy. And the purpose God gave you was never meant to be small enough to fit inside someone else's expectations.

You weren't sent by the crowd.

You were not commissioned by their applause or sustained by their agreement. Your purpose was not born in their approval, and it will not die in their rejection.

You were sent by God.

Before the stage, before the affirmation, before the doubt—you were called. Not to charm, but to change. Not to blend in, but to bear witness. Not to be accepted, but to be *faithful*.

And faithfulness will always ask more of you than popularity ever will.

So lift your eyes.

Look past the numbers, the nods, the silence, the praise. Look beyond the room, the platform, the image. Look to the One who named you, formed you, and still walks beside you.

You don't belong to public opinion.

You belong to the Presence that *saw you before you spoke a word.*

So reach—

Not for attention, but for alignment.

Not for applause, but for *assignment.*

You do not have to be loud to be true.

You do not have to be liked to be faithful.

You do not have to be seen to be sent.

Be bold, but not brash.

Be faithful, even when no one notices.

Be whole, even when you're misunderstood.

Let your voice be shaped in the secret place, not by the echo of approval.

Let your purpose stretch beyond performance and into something *eternal.*

The world may not celebrate you. But heaven already knows your name.

And that, dear child, is enough.

With clarity and courage,

—*Abba*

LETTER 7: COURAGE IS A CONVERSATION

A Father's Letters from the Wilderness of Calling

My Beloved Jeremiah,

Courage doesn't always look like what people think.
It isn't always loud. It doesn't always roar.
Sometimes it whispers. Sometimes it waits.
Sometimes courage isn't the moment you step
forward, but the moment you *stay*—when
everything in you says run, but your spirit says, *not
yet*.

We often imagine courage as something external.
Something visible. Something others can applaud.
But more often than not, it begins in silence—in
that sacred space where fear and faith meet and
wrestle for the same breath.

That's where courage is born.

Not in the absence of fear, but in the presence of
God.

In the honest conversation between your trembling soul and the One who called you anyway.

Before you stand before people, you must sit with Him.

Before you speak, you must listen.

Before you act, you must *ask*.

This is where real strength takes root—

in *conversation*, not in performance.

Jeremiah didn't become courageous because he was fearless.

He became courageous because he kept *coming back*.

He questioned. He complained. He wept. He argued. He even tried to quit. But he never stopped talking to God. That's what made him bold—not perfection, not poise, but proximity.

His courage was conversational.

He brought his fear into the presence of God, again and again.

He brought his weariness. His outrage. His hesitation.

And God didn't turn him away.

This is where true courage lives—not in bravado, but in return.

In the willingness to keep showing up in prayer, even when you're exhausted. Even when your heart is heavy. Even when your faith feels thin.

Courage grows every time you say, *"I don't know if I can do this,"* and God responds, *"I will be with you."* And somehow, in that rhythm of honesty and presence, you rise.

Do not despise your fear.

It does not mean you are unworthy. It does not mean you are weak. It simply means you are aware of the weight you carry—and that you care deeply about getting it right.

Fear is not your disqualification.

It is your invitation.

An invitation to return. To sit again with God in the quiet. To speak plainly. To ask the hard questions you've been too polite to say aloud. He can take it. He already knows.

Bring Him your trembling.

Bring Him the speech you don't feel ready to give.

Bring Him the decision you keep postponing.

Bring Him the face you're afraid to confront.

Bring Him the voice in your own head that

says, *You're not enough.*

And listen.

Not for thunder, but for truth.

Not for approval, but for presence.

Even your questions are a kind of prayer.

Even your doubts are evidence that you're still

listening.

Still reaching. Still *in it.*

And that, my child, is courage.

Make space for the conversation.

Not a performance. Not a ritual for its own sake.

But a steady, sacred rhythm of returning—again and

again—to the One who knows what He placed

inside you.

You don't need the perfect words. You don't need to

sound brave. You don't even need to be certain. You

just need to *show up.*

Every day if you can.

Every moment you remember.

A whisper in your car. A breath before the meeting.

A stillness before you sleep.

Let it be messy. Let it be simple. Let it be yours.

Because courage is not forged in the spotlight. It's grown in secret places—where honesty has room to breathe, and you can remember that you are not walking into any room alone.

Conversation with God is not preparation for the real thing.

It is the real thing.

Everything else flows from there.

So keep coming back.

Even if your voice shakes.

Even if all you have is silence.

Even if you don't know what to say.

God is not looking for polished speeches. He is looking for *presence.*

And every time you return, He meets you there— not with shame, but with strength.

Let courage grow in the quiet.

Let it be formed in questions, not just answers.

Let it rise from intimacy, not image.

You don't have to roar to be brave.

You just have to *respond.*

And if all you can say is, *"Here I am,"*

that is enough for God to begin again.

With steady grace,

—*Abba*

LETTER 8: TEAR DOWN AND BUILD UP

A Father's Letters from the Wilderness of Calling

My Beloved Jeremiah,

Some assignments don't begin with building.

They begin with *breaking*.

God does not always call us to create first.

Sometimes, He calls us to confront—to pull down, to uproot, to clear the ground before anything can grow. And that kind of work is holy, but it is also hard.

Because most people welcome what builds.

They celebrate the planting, the progress, the promise of something new.

But they rarely understand the tearing down.

You will be called not only to nurture, but to disrupt.

Not only to comfort, but to challenge.

Not only to construct, but to clear what was never meant to stand.

And that tension—the ache of it—will stay with
you.

You will feel it every time you speak what must be
said, knowing it might undo something familiar.
You will feel it every time you obey, even when your
obedience is misunderstood as destruction.

This was the call spoken over you from the
beginning:

*"See, today I appoint you over nations and kingdoms to
uproot and tear down, to destroy and overthrow, to
build and to plant."*

All six verbs matter.

But the first four are disruptive.

And the last two come later.

That's the rhythm of restoration.

Before anything can be planted, the soil must be
cleared. Before the foundation can be laid, the ruins
must be removed. Before something beautiful can
rise, the false and the fragile must fall.

This is not cruelty. It is mercy.

God does not call you to tear down for the sake of tearing down. He calls you to remove what is diseased, to dismantle what is built on lies, to make space for what is *true*.

It may look like destruction.

But it is preparation.

It is healing.

It is the beginning of something better.

But even when you know it's right, it won't feel easy.

There is a grief that comes with tearing down—especially when others only saw the surface. You'll be called divisive when you're simply discerning. You'll be seen as disrespectful when you're simply *obedient*. You may even feel isolated by the very people you hoped to serve.

And that loneliness? That ache of being misunderstood? It's real.

You will carry the weight of what others won't name.

You will grieve things they're still clinging to.

47

You will hear, *"Why would you disrupt this?"* when your heart is crying, *"Because it's already broken."*

You'll want to explain.

You'll want them to see what you see.

And sometimes, they won't.

That's part of the cost.

And still—*you must go forward.*

Because obedience does not always come with agreement. And healing rarely comes without disruption.

But hear me—this is not where the story ends.

You were not called only to tear down. You were also called to *build.* To *plant.* To bring forth something new and rooted and lasting. God never leaves the ground empty. He never removes without preparing to restore.

Yes, there will be dust. There will be silence. There may even be delay.

But beneath that cleared ground, the soil is being readied.

And in time, what once looked barren will bloom.

48

The same hands that pulled down will also lay the foundation.

The same voice that spoke correction will one day speak *hope*.

And the same heart that ached through loss will rejoice in what rises.

So do not lose heart in the middle.

The process is not punishment.

It is preparation.

And your role is not just to disrupt—it is to *redeem* what others thought was beyond repair.

So take up your tools, child.

Not just the hammer, but the seed.

Not just the courage to confront, but the compassion to rebuild.

Not just the voice that names what must fall, but the vision to see what can rise.

You are both disruptor *and* restorer.

Both prophet *and* planter.

Trust the timing.

Even when it's slow.

Even when it's lonely.

Even when it costs you more than it confirms you.

Keep working.

Keep speaking.

Keep believing that what God uproots, He intends
to renew.

And when the ground feels barren, remember—
there are things breaking forth beneath the surface
you cannot yet see.

With strength and tenderness,

—*Abba*

PART 3

TRUSTING THE LONG BLOOM

Waiting, Watching, and Becoming the Message

LETTER 9: WATCH THE ALMOND TREE

A Father's Letters from the Far Country of Faith

My Beloved Jeremiah,

There is a quiet wonder in the almond tree.

It does not shout its significance. It does not demand the season to speed up. But when all else is still bare—when winter still lingers in the bones of the earth—the almond tree begins to bloom.

It is the first to awaken. The first to show signs of life. The first to remind us that something is coming, even when nothing else seems ready.

That is why God showed it to you.

Not as decoration, but as declaration.

"What do you see, Jeremiah?" He asked.

And you answered, *"I see the branch of an almond tree."*

Then the Lord said, *"You have seen correctly, for I am watching to see that My word is fulfilled."*

This was no random image. It was a whisper in wood and bloom: *I am paying attention. I have not forgotten. My timing is unfolding, even when nothing else has yet caught up.*

The almond tree reminds us that God is not slow— He is *watching*.

He sees before we do. Moves before we notice. Speaks before we're ready to hear. His work begins beneath the surface, in silence, in sacred preparation. And when it appears, it often feels too early—or too subtle—to make sense.

But that's how faith grows.

While we wait for dramatic signs, God sends almond branches. Quiet affirmations. Small shifts. First fruits. And we are left with a choice: trust His watching, or demand our own pace.

We long for quick harvests.

He invites us into *watchfulness*.

We want immediate results.

He gives us early signs.

Because His Word doesn't rush.

It *ripens*.

And if we are paying attention, we'll see that He's already begun.

We often mistake *delay* for *absence*.

We assume that if we don't see immediate progress, nothing is happening. If the promise hasn't blossomed by now, it must have been withdrawn. If doors don't open, or results don't come, or answers don't arrive—we begin to question if God is still near.

But the almond branch invites us to look again.

It is small. Unassuming. Quiet. But it speaks volumes to those who are listening.

It says: *I am still watching.*

I have not forgotten.

The Word is working, even now.

And if we learn to see as God sees—to value the early bloom instead of resenting the slow season— we will begin to recognize His faithfulness not only in the harvest, but in the hint.

Because what looks like "not yet" is often *already beginning.*

The almond tree does not force the season.

It simply watches—and responds.

That, too, is your calling.

Not to control the timing.

Not to manufacture the outcome.

But to become *watchful*.

Pay attention to what God is doing in small places.

Notice the early signs. The quiet nudges. The almost imperceptible ways the Word is already stretching toward fulfillment.

You don't need to understand the whole picture to trust that something sacred is unfolding.

Be still enough to perceive it.

Be patient enough to let it bloom.

What God starts, He watches.

What He watches, He waters.

And what He waters—*in time*—He brings to fruit.

The branch has already budded. The process has already begun.

And your part is not to rush it, but to *remain present to it*.

So lift your eyes, beloved.

Even if the ground still looks bare.

Even if winter seems unending.

Even if no one else sees what you see.

Watch the almond tree.

Let it remind you that God is still watching. Still working. Still bringing things to life in ways that don't always announce themselves.

Do not be discouraged by the slowness of the season.

Do not despise the signs because they are small.

He who began the Word in you is watching over it still.

And He will be faithful to bring it to bloom.

So wait—not in worry, but in wonder.

Watch—not for the dramatic, but for the divine.

The branch has budded.

The promise is near.

The Word is alive.

And God is *still watching*.

With patience and peace,

—*Abba*

LETTER 10: FAITH BEYOND FEELINGS

A Father's Letters from the Far Country of Faith

My Beloved Jeremiah,

There will be days when your faith doesn't feel like fire.

Days when the sky is quiet. When prayer feels like reaching into fog. When obedience doesn't stir your heart, and worship feels more like discipline than delight.

There will be mornings when the weight of calling seems too heavy to lift, and nights when you wonder if anything you're doing still matters.

The presence of God will feel distant—*not absent*, but hard to find.

And you will question yourself. You will wonder if something is wrong. You will revisit every decision, every word, every moment that once felt certain, and ask, *Why can't I feel it anymore?*

This is not failure.

This is *formation*.

The path of faith is not always paved with clarity.
Sometimes it is built in the dark, by trust alone.
The absence of feeling is not the absence of God.
It is the invitation to *grow roots*—to anchor your
faith not in emotion, but in truth. Not in how God
feels, but in who God is.

You are not going backward when the fire dims. You
are being invited into something more stable.
Something more mature. Something
more *durable* than inspiration.

This is where faith deepens—beneath the surface,
beneath the noise, beneath the thrill. It matures
when the scaffolding of sensation falls away, and
what's left is trust.

And trust, unlike feeling, does not need to be
constant. It only needs to be *true*.

You will not always feel called.

You will not always feel seen.

You will not always feel strong.

But you are still all of these things—because God's
Word is not governed by your emotions.

It was true before you felt it.

It remains true when you don't.

So keep walking.

Even when the fire feels like an ember. Even when your prayers are quiet, your worship is weary, and your spirit feels dry.

Because these are the moments that count the most.

These are the days when faith becomes real—not because you feel full, but because you remain *faithful*. Not because you're overflowing with conviction, but because you choose to show up anyway.

Do not despise these ordinary acts of trust.

The quiet prayer. The opened scripture. The steady "yes."

They are not small. They are sacred.

Because in these hidden places, your roots grow deeper. Your soul learns that faith is not a sensation—it's a decision. A returning. A remembering.

This is the courage of the called: to believe when belief doesn't feel electric.

To stay when you feel like slipping away.

To love even when you feel unloved.

And in doing so, you become something steady in a world that keeps shifting.

And while you're holding on, know this: *God is holding you.*

He has not disappeared. He has not gone silent. He has not withheld Himself to punish you. He is still present—*even here.*

Still speaking.

Still sustaining.

Still watching over His word to perform it.

His closeness is not always loud. It is not always felt. But it is never absent.

You are not abandoned because you feel dry.

You are not forgotten because you feel nothing.

You are not unfaithful because your heart isn't stirred like it once was.

Sometimes God draws near in ways we cannot sense.

Sometimes He's quiet because He is strengthening what cannot be shaken.

And if you listen—not with your emotions, but with your spirit—you will know: *He is still with you.*

So keep showing up.

Even in the silence.

Even in the stillness.

Even in the in-between where the fire flickers low.

You are not powered by passion alone.

You are sustained by *faithfulness*—not yours, but God's.

He is still writing your story.

Still watering what you planted in hope.

Still honoring the "yes" you whispered when your soul was trembling.

You are not forgotten.

You are not off course.

You are not disqualified because you feel dry.

You are still chosen.

Still called.

Still *His*.

So take the next step.

Say the next prayer.

Speak the next truth.

And trust that even this quiet stretch is holy ground.

With calm assurance,

—*Abba*

FINAL LETTER: YOU WERE ALWAYS THE MESSAGE

A Father's Letters from the Far Country of Faith

My Beloved Jeremiah,

If you are reading this now, you've already come farther than you think.

Not because the path has been easy, but because you've kept walking—even when the road was silent. Even when your heart was heavy. Even when you weren't sure if any of this would ever matter. You have made it through questions and seasons, through fire and fog, through the ache of calling and the stillness of waiting. And while I cannot know where you are as these words meet you, I do know this:

The journey was never just about the message you would speak.

It was about the one you would *become*.

Because the truth is—*you were always the message.*

Long before you crafted a sermon or wrote a line or spoke with boldness, your very life was speaking something holy. Your presence in the world, your persistence through pain, your return to God again and again—it all carries a word that cannot be silenced.

You may not have realized it, but your faithfulness—quiet, unfinished, sometimes unsure— has been the most powerful word you've ever spoken.

Not because it was perfect.

Not because it was loud.

But because it was *true*.

Every time you showed up when it would've been easier to disappear.

Every time you prayed without answers.

Every time you stood in truth when no one applauded.

Every time you chose love over recognition, integrity over approval, return over retreat—*you were preaching*.

Final Letter

You were preaching without a pulpit.

You were proclaiming without a platform.

You were revealing God's heart simply by being faithful to what He placed in yours.

And I am proud of you. Not just for what you've done, but for who you're becoming.

That becoming—that slow, holy becoming—is the message.

And it is more than enough.

You may not feel ready.

You may still carry questions.

But readiness was never a requirement for calling. Willingness is.

And you have shown that—even in silence, even in shadow—you have been willing to walk, to wrestle, to return. And now, my dear child, it is time to trust what's already been placed in you.

Not because the road ahead will be easy.

Not because every word will come without trembling.

But because you are no longer walking from a place

of trying to prove something.

You are walking from a place of *truth*.

The message lives in you now.

Not just in your voice, but in your presence.

Not just in your wisdom, but in your wounds.

Not just in your clarity, but in your courage to keep showing up.

So go—not to impress, but to embody.

Not to be great, but to be *faithful*.

And trust that what God began, He is still watching over.

So may you go—

not as one trying to become something,

but as one who has *already been named*.

May your steps carry truth,

even when your voice cannot.

May your wounds speak healing,

even when your words feel small.

May your presence preach the faithfulness of God,

even when no one is watching.

Final Letter

You are the message, beloved.

And now, you are also the messenger.

Walk slowly.

Walk honestly.

Walk boldly.

And remember:

you were never sent to prove anything.

You were sent to *embody* something.

And that, dear child, is more than enough.

With a full heart,

—*Abba*

WHEN THE LETTERS ARE DONE

Closing Note/Afterword

You've made it to the final page, but the real work doesn't end here.

You've walked through silence and fire, through names remembered and names reclaimed. You've wept beside prophets and risen with questions still in your hands. And still—you are here.

That alone is worth blessing.

These letters were never the destination. They were a lantern for the road, a voice in the wilderness, a father's echo into the still places where so many of us wrestle. They were not written to give you a script, but to give you *space*—to feel, to listen, to return.

If anything has stirred, if anything has softened, if even a single line made you pause—then the letters have done their work.

Because the real message has never been mine.

It has always been *yours*.

You carry it now—not in paragraphs, but in
presence. In the choices you make when no one sees.
In the quiet "yes" you whisper to God when you're
unsure. In the fire you still tend, even when it
doesn't roar.

You are not just the recipient of these words.

You are the continuation of them.

So go on—

not as someone who must perform,

but as someone who is becoming.

And if ever you forget what you carry—

return.

Read again.

Watch the almond tree.

Feel the fire.

Listen for the voice that called you by name.

And remember:

You were always the message.

Benediction

May the fire in your bones never be mistaken for
failure.
May the silence between your prayers be filled with
presence.
May your fear remind you of how deeply you care.
And may your faith remind you of how faithfully
you are held.

When the path is quiet, may you keep walking.
When the calling is costly, may you keep standing.
And when the world forgets your name,
may you remember the One who never has.

Go with your name intact.
Go with truth in your hands.
Go with your soul rooted in the Word that still lives
in you.

You are not just sent.
You are seen.
You are not just carrying a message.
You are the message.

And for the road ahead,
that will be enough.

APPENDIX

Scripture & Thematic Index

Selected Scriptures

Scripture	Theme	Referenced In
Jeremiah 1:4–10	Calling, formation, fear, voice	Letters 1, 2, 3, 4, 8
Jeremiah 1:12	Divine attentiveness	Letter 9
Jeremiah 20:9	Prophetic fire, frustration	Letter 4
Psalm 139:13–16	Being known, identity	Letter 1
1 Samuel 16:7	Internal worth over appearances	Letter 2
2 Timothy 1:7	Courage, divine empowerment	Letters 2, 7
Isaiah 43:1–2	Identity, being named, presence	Letters 1, 10
Matthew 10:19–20	God's presence in speaking	Letters 6, 7
Lamentations 3:26	Waiting in silence	Letter 9
Galatians 6:9	Endurance, not giving up	Letters 5, 10
Philippians 1:6	God completing His work	Final Letter
Romans 8:24–25	Hope in the unseen	Letters 9, 10
Isaiah 61:1–3	Liberated to liberate	Letter 10, Final Letter

Key Themes

Theme	Explored In Letters
Identity	1 (*Before You Were You*), 3 (*What's in a Name?*), 10
Fear & Courage	2, 4, 5, 6, 7, 10
Calling	1, 2, 4, 5, 6, 8, Final Letter
Fire & Frustration	4, 5
Popularity & Purpose	6
Conversation & Prayer	7
Breaking & Building	8
Watching & Waiting	9
Endurance	5, 10
Silence & Presence	9, 10
Becoming the Message	Final Letter
Restoration	8, Final Letter

About the Author

Bishop Eric J. Freeman, Ph.D., is a pastor, author,

theologian, and spiritual father whose ministry centers on voice, identity, and the Gospel's power to call people into courageous, incarnational purpose. He is the founding pastor of The Meeting Place Church of Greater Columbia and serves as a teacher, preacher, and cultural bridge-builder.

His scholarly and pastoral work explores themes of calling, endurance, and sacred voice—especially among those who have felt unseen or silenced. He is the author of *Grimké's Gospel Echo: A Handbook for Preaching, Clear Faith: Eight Simple Truths Every Christian Should Know*, a doctrinal primer for spiritually grounded living, and *Break Every Chain: A Revolutionary Journey to Emancipation*, a 21-day devotional workbook guiding believers through spiritual liberation and practical freedom in Christ.

Letters of a Father to His Son Jeremiah—A Spiritual Journey to Meaning, Purpose, and Identity is his most personal work to date—born from letters never sent and prayers still unfolding.

He continues to write and speak to those still walking their callings out slowly, faithfully, and with fire.

The
Freeman
Institute
FOR INTEGRATIVE RESEARCH

www.ingramcontent.com/pod-product-compliance
Lightning Source LLC
Chambersburg PA
CBHW022009100426
42736CB00041B/1294